The
Apple Pie Alien

Other Orchard Storybooks

Clipper Street Stories by Bernard Ashley
CALLING FOR SAM
TALLER THAN BEFORE

Jupiter Jane Stories by Sheila Lavelle
THE BOGGY BAY MARATHON

Woodside School Stories by Jean Ure
THE FRIGHT
WHO'S TALKING?

A JUPITER JANE STORY

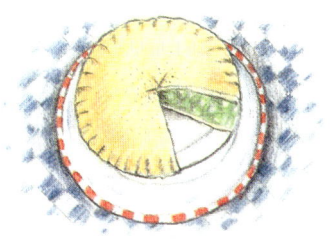

The
Apple Pie Alien

Sheila Lavelle

Illustrated by
Emma Crosby

ORCHARD BOOKS
London

Text copyright © Sheila Lavelle 1987
Illustrations copyright © Emma Crosby 1987
First published in Great Britain in 1987 by
ORCHARD BOOKS
10 Golden Square, London W1R 3AF
Orchard Books Australia
14 Mars Road, Lane Cove NSW 2066
Orchard Books Canada
20 Torbay Road, Markham, Ontario 23P 1G6
1 85213 081 4
Printed in Great Britain
by A. Wheaton, Exeter

1

Katy Stuart didn't want to share her bedroom with some weird monster from outer space with two heads and lumpy green skin. The very idea made her hopping mad.

It was Katy's dad who had started it all, after seeing that advertisement in the morning paper. He was eating his breakfast at the time, and he was so astonished that his glasses slid off his nose into his bowl of cornflakes.

"Here, Maggie, listen to this," he said to his wife, licking the milk off the lenses. "'English family wanted, with large garden, and lake or pool, to take care of young female visitor from the planet Jupiter. Last two weeks in July.'"

"Don't talk with your mouth full," said Mrs Stuart, banging the coffee pot down so hard that the lid rattled. "And don't read the newspaper at the table. It's very rude." She stared at him suddenly. "Visitor from where, did you say?"

Mr Stuart was so used to his wife's nagging that it no longer had any effect. He spooned up another mouthful of cornflakes and peered again at the paper.

"Jupiter," he said, munching. "The planet Jupiter. That's what it says."

Katy let in Tommy, the ginger cat, who was mewing at the door.

"It must be one of those exchange visits," she said, sitting down at the table. "You know, to learn the language and stuff. Betty Bugle had a French girl to stay last holidays."

Mrs Stuart turned her mouth down at the corners as if her coffee tasted of vinegar. "Yes," she said sourly. "And what a disaster it was, too. The kid broke three windows and set fire to the curtains. They sent her back after a week before she wrecked the whole house. I don't want anybody like that here, thank you very much." She stabbed at her boiled egg as if it were about to leap up and bite her.

"Well, I think it would be very interesting," said Mr Stuart, putting sugar lumps into the milk jug by mistake. "A little visitor would be a bit of company for Katy in the school holidays, and she could share Katy's room."

Katy's heart sank. Her bedroom was the only place where she could get any peace, and she loved to be by herself with her books and her pop music and her watercolour paints. Anyway, this was the craziest thing she had ever heard of. Goodness knows what sort of creature could turn up. What if it wasn't even house-trained and made puddles on the carpet like Mrs Morgan's dog?

"Aw, Dad. It's a rotten idea," she said, making a face as if her stomach ached. "You know I hate sharing my room. And we can't take any weird creature to Grandma's. I can't see Gran getting on with a space monster at all."

"We're not going to Grandma's until August," Katy's dad pointed out. "That's no problem."

Mrs Stuart got up and began to clear the table, scraping the scraps into a bowl for the cat.

"Get a move on, you two," she said briskly. "And you can forget the whole thing. We have got a large garden, if you can call that jungle out there a garden. But we certainly haven't got a lake or pool."

Katy's spirits rose at once, but fell again when her dad refused to be put off.

"What about that lovely fish pond I made?" he protested. "That's a sort of pool, isn't it?" He looked hurt as his wife snorted down her nose in disgust.

"Fish pond?" she said, carrying dishes to the sink. "It's more like a mud bath. The garden gnome fell in last week and we haven't seen him since." She turned the taps full on so that she wouldn't hear any more of his nonsense.

"Maybe it's just a hoax, Dad," said Katy, putting her arm round him and pressing her cheek to his, so that his aftershave tickled her nose and made her sneeze. "There's supposed to be no life on Jupiter. It's all liquid and gas."

"Like your dad, when he's had a few beers," said Katy's mum, with another loud snort.

Mr Stuart took a pen and writing paper from the dresser drawer. Normally a mild, quiet man, he could be very stubborn once he got an idea into his head.

"Well, I'm going to find out," he said. "There's no harm in that, is there?"

And so that was why there they all were, shivering in the garden in the rain at midnight six weeks later, on a wet, chilly night in the middle of July. A ring of Christmas tree fairy lights surrounded the lawn, winking prettily in the raindrops, but they did nothing to cheer Katy up. She stared anxiously up at the sky, and a feeling of dread filled her chest like a lump of cold porridge.

Mr Stuart looked at his watch. "Shouldn't be long now," he muttered shakily, and Katy realised with a small shock that he was scared, too. "They said twelve o'clock. Hope these lights are all right."

His letter to the Inter-planetary Relations Board, sent to a box number address in London, had received a prompt reply. He had been thanked for his kind offer and informed of the date and time of the visitor's arrival. And he had been asked to place a ring of lights in the garden, in a circle twenty metres across, to guide the spaceship to the ground. It had been Katy who had borrowed all the Christmas tree lights from everybody in the street, and her request had caused a few raised eyebrows since she could hardly explain what they were for.

"I hope the creature hasn't got fleas or anything," grumbled Katy's mum, pulling up the collar of her raincoat. "And I hope it doesn't trek mud in on my good carpets. I don't know why I agreed to all this. We must all be soft in the head."

Then they all gasped and clutched at one another as a bright green glow suddenly appeared in the sky above them. Katy's stomach did a sort of wild somersault, and for a moment she thought her heart was going to jump right out of her mouth. She swallowed hard and stared with round eyes.

It wasn't easy to make out in the rain, but the green glow seemed to be hovering over the garden. Then, while they watched, it slowly faded and a small, oval-shaped, silvery object floated silently to the ground in the very centre of the ring of lights.

"Good lord," said Katy's dad faintly. "It's no bigger than a bath tub."

"Maybe they're midgets," whispered Mrs Stuart.

"Maybe they're frogs," said Katy, thinking of the lake or pool.

There was a dead silence for a moment and nobody dared to breathe. Then a small hatch in the roof of the craft slid open and a cross voice rang out in the darkness.

"What rotten, lousy weather! I

hope my supper's ready. I'm starving!"

Mr Stuart switched on his torch and they all gaped at the figure scrambling out of the open hatch.

It wasn't a two-headed monster with lumpy green skin. It wasn't a midget with fleas. And it certainly wasn't a frog.

It was a very ordinary-looking

small girl of about Katy's age, with a freckled face and fair hair done in skinny little pigtails. She wore a striped T-shirt and blue dungarees, and on her feet were a huge pair of rubber boots.

"Hi, everybody," she said, plodding towards them over the grass. "I'm Jane, from Jupiter."

Katy didn't know whether to be relieved or disappointed. So she began to laugh instead.

And that was Katy's first mistake.

2

Jupiter Jane stared round the kitchen as if she'd never seen one before. "What are all those funny things?" she asked, pointing.

Mrs Stuart smiled proudly. "Fridge, washing machine, tumble dryer," she said, patting each one fondly as if it were a pet poodle. "I don't suppose you have things like these where you come from?"

"Only in museums," said Jane, pulling a notebook and pencil from her pocket and making a few notes. Katy gave a little snort of laughter, but turned it into a cough when she saw her mother's face.

Mrs Stuart's mouth opened and closed like a haddock out of water, but she said nothing. She banged a pan on the stove, switched on the toaster, and prepared a hasty meal for the visitor.

Jane sat at the kitchen table and scowled at the two poached eggs on toast as if they had been seasoned with arsenic.

"They warned me you'd laugh at my boots," she muttered, in a sulky voice. "But nobody said I'd get dead animals to eat. Haven't you got anything else?"

"I wasn't laughing at your boots, honest," said Katy wearily, for the third time. "I just wasn't expecting a human being, that's all."

Jane pushed the plate away and looked at Katy as if she were something smelly stuck to her shoe.

"I suppose you thought I'd be a two-headed monster with green skin," she said crossly. "We're all human on Jupiter, if you must know. And on Mars. And on Saturn. And on all the other planets. So there."

Katy sighed. Things had got off to a bad start, and the visitor had fallen out with her already. As if she cared about the stupid boots, anyway. It was going to be a horrible two weeks if they all went on like this.

"It's not dead animals; it's poached eggs," said Mrs Stuart, her lips pressed in a thin line as if they were zipped together. "And I'd rather you took those boots off indoors, if you don't mind."

"I'll keep them on, thank you," said Jane in a don't-argue-with-me sort of voice. "And don't you know that eggs are baby chickens? You people must be more backward than we thought."

Out came the notebook again and she scribbled for a moment. Then she got up, opened the fridge door, and helped herself to a large slice of apple pie.

"This'll have to do, I suppose," she said, taking a bite. "Although it's not much after a three-day journey through space." Her eyes widened in surprise as she swallowed the first mouthful. "Your husband makes very good apple pie, Mrs Stuart," she said, licking her fingers. "I think I'll have some more." She took the whole pie out of the fridge and, to Katy's disgust, greedily scoffed the lot.

"Mr Stuart can't even boil the kettle without burning it," glowered Katy's mum. "I made the pie myself."

Jane gulped down another huge bite. "On Jupiter it's my Dad who does the cooking," she said. "My mum goes out to work."

She scraped the plate noisily and then leaned back with a satisfied sigh. "Now, where am I supposed to sleep?" she said. "And where's Katy's father with my luggage?"

Mr Stuart struggled through the door with a large metal box with handles, tripping over the rug as he did so.

"Be careful!" shouted Jane, leaping out of her chair. "My computer's in there! I can't get home without that!"

"Sorry, dear," said Mr Stuart mildly. "I'll take it upstairs for you. You'll be sharing Katy's bedroom."

Jane's face turned pale. "Oh, no!" she said quickly. "I can't do that. I must have a room to myself. I really must."

Katy stared at her curiously. "I'll sleep on the sofa in the living-room, if you like," she offered. The kid was welcome to the room, if it meant that much to her, Katy thought.

Mrs Stuart was shaking her head, grim-faced.

"You'll do nothing of the kind," she snapped. "There's a perfectly good spare bed made up for Jane, and that's where she'll sleep. Now, upstairs, both of you. It's well past your bedtime."

Jane's eyes turned grey and cold as winter. She went sullenly up the stairs, while Mr Stuart followed with the huge metal box, knocking holes in the wallpaper at every step.

"Sleep well, girls," he panted at the door, but Jupiter Jane turned her back on him and stared out of the window.

Katy changed into her pyjamas and went to brush her teeth in the bathroom. When she came back, Jane was still gazing out of the open window, fully dressed. The rain had stopped and the sky was filled with stars.

"Which one's Jupiter?" said Katy, hopping into bed, and trying to be friendly. But that was another mistake, for the stranger at once burst into tears.

"You can't even see it from here!" she wailed. "I want to go home!" And she flung herself face down on the bed and howled until she almost choked. "I didn't want to come to this rotten planet in the first place!" she sobbed into the pillows. "I wanted to go to Saturn with my friend Deborah!"

Katy didn't know what to do. "Come on, Jane," she said, when the sobs had died down slightly. "Get into bed. Maybe you'll feel better in the morning."

Jane sat up and blew her nose on a corner of the bedspread. She stared at Katy for a moment, hiccupping and rubbing her eyes. Then she went to her box and rummaged about in it until she found a long pink nightdress.

"All right," she said, starting to undress. "But I'll have to take my boots off. And you'd better not start laughing at my feet."

"Why should I?" said Katy, wondering what all the fuss was about.

But when Jane pulled off the big rubber boots and flung them defiantly into a corner of the bedroom, Katy didn't feel like laughing at all. All she felt was shock and amazement, for she had never seen feet like these in her life.

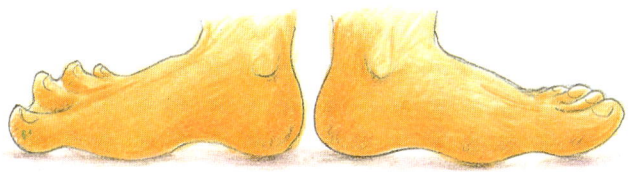

Jane's feet were enormous. Almost the size of dinner plates. They were bright orange in colour, as if she'd been paddling in paint. And the toes were webbed.

Katy gulped. "I don't think they're at all f...funny," she managed to stammer. "They...they're probably very useful."

"Oh, they are," said Jane, cheering up at once. "Just wait until tomorrow, when you show me your lake. You'll see what a good swimmer I am." She gave Katy a suspicious look. "You have got a lake, I hope?"

Katy thought of the slimy fish pond and felt her face turn red. "Well, it's not really a lake," she said, "More like a sort of pond, I suppose."

Jane slid under the covers and grinned at Katy. "That's all right," she said. "As long as it's big enough to swim in. I'll get ill if I don't swim every day. The planet Jupiter is mostly water, you see, except for all the tiny islands inhabited by us humans. So we've developed feet like these to survive. Just like Mars humans have all got big ears, to keep themselves cool in all that heat..."

Her voice tailed off in a sort of gasp, and Katy saw that she was staring at the doorway, her mouth opening wide with fright.

Tommy, the ginger cat, was padding softly round the edge of the door, yawning sleepily and showing all his teeth. He sharpened his claws briefly on the carpet, then stalked over to the visitor's bed, sniffed it curiously, and jumped lightly onto the bedspread.

Jane screamed and flung herself off the bed against the wall. Her green eyes blazed red and gold for a few seconds, then she scrambled to her feet and pointed her right hand at the cat. The hand began to quiver and there was a sound like rushing wind. Then, while Katy watched in helpless horror, the astonished cat rose slowly into the air, sailed out through the open window into the garden, and landed with a crash among the rubbish bins.

"There!" gasped Jane, clutching her trembling fingers with her other hand. "That's got rid of that horrible creature. Quick, Katy, shut the window in case it comes back."

Furious shrieks, thumps and howls of rage brought Katy's parents bursting into the room. And Katy had to be dragged away by force to stop her from yanking those skinny little pigtails clean off Jane's head.

3

Katy's black eye throbbed painfully as she sat down to bacon and eggs in the kitchen the next morning. It was raining again and the weather matched the gloomy way she felt. She glared across the table at Jane, who seemed as fresh as a buttercup and none the worse for their fight.

The visitor had already been up for hours, poking into every room in the house, sniggering at everything she saw and making page after page of notes in her little blue notebook. She was now eating slices of freshly-baked apple pie with one hand, while drawing pictures of Katy's bathroom and its old-fashioned plumbing with the other. The lavatory had made her laugh out loud the first time she saw it, and she had made Mrs Stuart explain over and over again how it worked and where the water came from.

Katy's dad sat down at the table with a cup of tea. "Come on, Katy. Don't sulk," he said. "Let's all have a nice little chat." He stirred his tea with the butter-knife and peered down in surprise as blobs of grease floated to the top. "Ah, tea," he murmured. "The cup that cheers, when you've got no beers."

Katy didn't even smile. "I'd rather have a chat with an alligator," she scowled, pressing a cold spoon against her eye. "Poor old Tommy didn't half get a fright. He shot straight up the apple tree and still hasn't come down."

"What's an alligator?" said Jane, looking up, but Katy only scowled even harder and stuck out her tongue.

Katy's mum had got over the fit of hysterics she'd had the night before on first seeing those orange webbed feet. And since Jane had fixed the faulty microchip on the washing machine earlier that morning she was now firmly on the visitor's side. "Poor Jane got an even bigger fright," she said, slapping angrily at the floor around the table with a wet mop. "She thought Tommy was going to attack her. Didn't you, Jane?"

Jane swallowed the last of the pie and started on a jar of strawberry jam, scooping it out with a teaspoon. "We haven't got nasty creatures like cats on Jupiter," she told Katy with a toss of her pigtails. "There aren't any animals that kill things. Only birds, and rabbits, and goats and stuff. My ancestors took them in the first spaceships from Earth, ages and ages ago. When they first settled on the other planets."

Katy didn't believe a word of it. "That's stupid," she snorted. "I bet you're making it all up. You're probably just a Russian spy, and not from Jupiter at all. Everybody knows there's only dust and poison gas up there." She lifted her feet off the floor as her mother's wet mop came dangerously near.

Jane rubbed at the skin on her arms, which was beginning to look dry and cracked, like peeling suntan.

"Well, everybody's wrong, so there," she said, speaking in a bossy voice like Katy's teacher at school. "The air on the other planets is just as good as it is here. Millions of people live up there. On Mars, and Saturn, and Uranus, and on all those other places as well. And they all zoom around in all kinds of spaceships, visiting and trading with each other." She looked at Katy's father severely. "Earth people used to do the same, until you lot spoiled things by wanting to fight and have wars with everybody all the time."

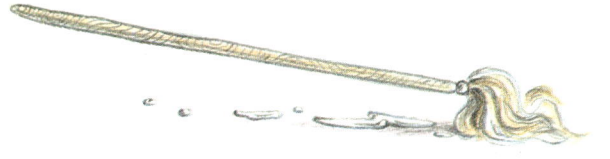

"We still haven't changed much," muttered Katy's dad, shaking splashes of water off his slippers. His wife finished mopping the floor and leaned the mop against the wall while she tipped the water down the sink.

"Everybody got fed up with you in the end," Jane went on, finishing the jam and opening a jar of honey. "So they all got together years ago and destroyed your spaceships. And all the designs and plans, so you couldn't make any more. Then they put these sort of screens round themselves. Space barriers, or something. To hide the real surface of the planets, and make them look as if nobody could live there."

"So that's why our scientists can only find dead worlds, with no life on them?" said Katy's dad. "Amazing!" He took his cup to the draining-board, skidding sideways on the wet mop and swearing as he banged his knee on a cupboard.

"What was that word?" asked Jane, reaching quickly for her notebook. Mr Stuart went pink and his wife glared at him angrily.

"Don't write it down, Jane," she said. "It's very rude. I've told him hundreds of times not to say it." She began to clear the table. "You haven't told us what you're here for, anyway," she said. "Is it a sort of holiday?"

"Holiday!" said Jane scornfully. "I'm not that stupid. Nobody ever comes here for a holiday." She carefully wrote the rude word down in her book. "No, I was sent here by the HCG," she said. "That's a sort of government on Jupiter. They've got some crazy idea that Earth humans might have changed... stopped squabbling so much, maybe. So a few of us kids have been sent to find out." She tapped her notebook. "I have to make a report. And I have to start making friends with your kids. Earth's future leaders."

"Making friends?" sneered Katy. "Huh! You'll have a war started in no time. How do you manage that trick with your fingers?"

Jane pushed away the empty honey jar. "It's a special sort of power," she said, pointing a quivering finger at the sugar bowl.

Katy's mouth dropped open as the bowl rose steadily into the air and floated across the room to the dresser. Mr Stuart gaped, and just managed to catch his glasses as they slid off the end of his nose.

"I can lift or move anything," boasted Jane. "Just by putting all my will-power into my fingers. It isn't half useful sometimes. All humans can do it, actually. Earth people have just forgotten how."

Katy's dad pointed a hopeful finger at his wife's back and looked disappointed when nothing happened.

"Well, you'd better not do it to my cat any more," glowered Katy. "Or I'll..."

The sugar bowl glided smoothly back towards the table and hovered for a moment just above Katy's head.

"You'll what?" grinned Jane, an

impish look in her strange green eyes.

"Nothing," said Katy through clenched teeth, and was relieved to see the sugar bowl come gently to rest on the table-cloth. Jane laughed out loud at Katy's furious expression.

"Come on, Grumpyface," she said. "Let's go and have a look at this pool of yours. I'll be all dried up if I don't get a swim soon." Scratching at her flaking skin, she ran out into the wet garden, leaving Katy and her father staring at one another in dismay.

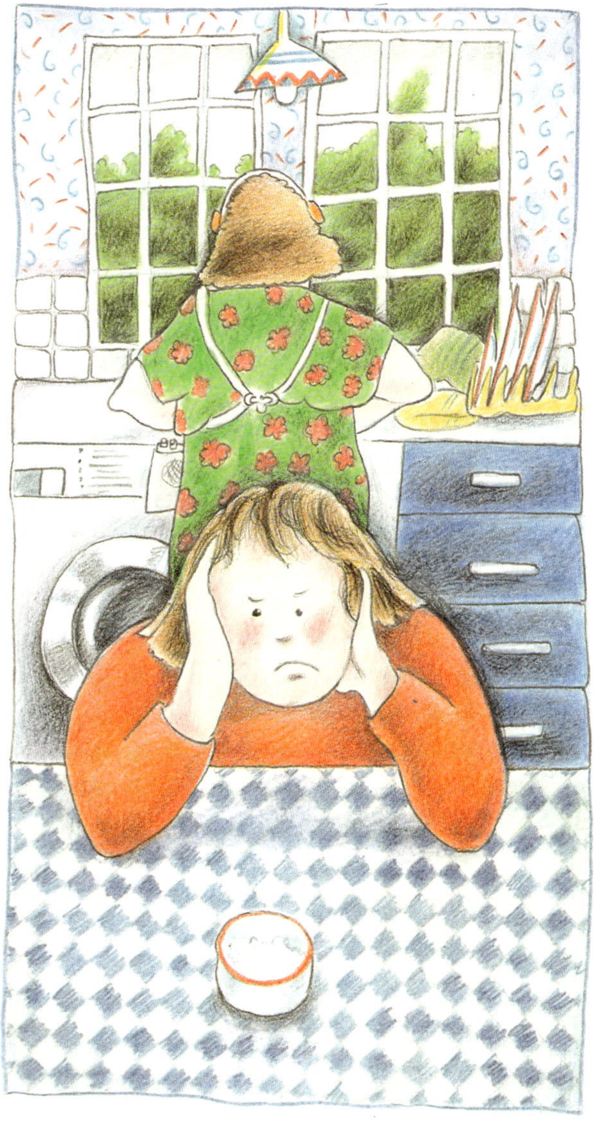

4

Nobody spoke for a long time, and the only sound came from Mrs Stuart clashing dishes together like cymbals in the sink. Katy blinked back a few angry tears.

"I'd better see what she's up to, I suppose," sighed Katy's dad at last. He got up and went outside.

Katy ran through the rain after him and pulled him round to face her.

"She's awful, Dad!" she burst out fiercely. "We can't put up with this for two whole weeks. I'm going to tell the horrible creature to clear off home."

Mr Stuart shook his head. "Give her a bit more time, Katy," he said. "Remember she's offering peace to everybody on Earth. Just think what it would mean if all the planets were friends again. Space travel...trade...wonderful new inventions..." He patted Katy's hand soothingly. "I know it's not easy, love," he said. "But if you could just try a bit harder..."

His voice faltered and then broke

off altogether as a rose tree in full bloom suddenly flew over his head, closely followed by a muddy garden gnome. Clumps of lupins and poppies went sailing past, showering Katy and her father with loose soil and pebbles.

"What the...what on earth...?" gasped Mr Stuart, clutching his glasses to his nose and racing off down the path with Katy after him. They skidded to a halt and stared wide-eyed at the scene in front of them.

At the bottom of the garden, where the fish pond with its edging of shrubs and flowers had once been, there was now an enormous hole. Soil and turf lay in heaps all over the lawn, and uprooted dahlias and marigolds draped every fence.

In the middle of the hole stood Jane, covered in dirt and mud. She was hopping gleefully from one foot to the other, and pointing the quivering fingers of her right hand at a water pipe which she had just uncovered.

"No! Stop!" shouted Katy's dad,

jumping up and down and waving his arms. "Leave that alone!" But he was too late. With a loud crack the pipe burst. Water gushed out in a torrent and rapidly began to fill the hole.

Jane turned and saw them. "Hi, Katy. Hi, Mr Stuart," she called. "I didn't think much of your smelly old pond. Come and see the lovely swimming pool I'm making for you. Wasn't I clever to find the pipe?" And she waded into the muddy water and began to splash about, a blissful expression on her face.

Katy and her father watched in stunned silence as the level of water rose higher and higher. As soon as it was deep enough, Jane gave a cry of delight and dived under the surface with all her clothes on. Katy's dad wiped the raindrops off his glasses.

"I'd better go and phone the Water Board," he said in a dazed voice. "The whole street will be flooded at this rate." He hurried back to the house, trampling through the rhubarb patch in his haste.

Katy stood in the rain watching the flash of Jane's orange feet as they appeared now and then near the surface of the pool. She's really done it now, thought Katy. Even Dad won't want her to stay after this.

Then a faint mew made her look up. A familiar ginger figure was crawling unsteadily towards her along one of the branches of the apple tree. Katy's heart gave a lurch when she saw that the trunk of the tree was now entirely surrounded by water.

"Wait!" she called, her knees turning wobbly with fright. "Hang on! You'll fall...!" Her voice rose to a squeak as the thin branch began to bend under Tommy's weight. His feet lost their grip and slithered sideways. He hung for a moment with his hind claws scrabbling at the air, then down he tumbled out of the tree to land with a splash in the pond.

"Tommy!" wailed Katy, running up and down the edge and wishing desperately that she had learnt to swim. Then Tommy's small wet head popped up, with his two front paws paddling away like mad. Beside him in the water Katy saw the freckled face and dripping pigtails of Jupiter Jane.

"Hey!" Jane shouted. "Your cat likes the pool. Why don't you come in too?"

Katy's voice seemed to be stuck in her throat.

"Get him out!" she managed to stammer at last. "He can't swim!"

"He is swimming," said Jane, circling round the struggling cat. "Maybe he's not enjoying it much, though." Katy almost sobbed with relief as Jane scooped Tommy up in her arms and swam towards her.

"He's all right, Katy," said Jane, holding him up out of the water. "Just a bit wet, that's all."

"He almost got drowned!" cried Katy furiously. "And it's all your fault! Just clear off back to Jupiter where you came from, will you? And the sooner the better!" She reached out to snatch the soggy bundle from Jane's outstretched hands.

And then it happened. Katy's foot skidded sideways on the

muddy slope and she somehow lost her balance. Before she could do anything to stop herself, down she slipped into the pool and the cold water closed over her head.

Katy sat on the living-room sofa wrapped in a blanket, sipping hot chocolate with a teaspoon of brandy in it. A damp but purring Tommy lay curled up in her lap.

Jane, convinced that she would be blamed for Katy's accident, had scrambled into dry clothes and hurriedly packed her luggage. She had wheeled the little spaceship into the garage out of the rain, and was now checking over the controls with her portable computer. As soon as it got dark she would be gone, thought Katy. And good riddance to bad rubbish.

Katy's dad came in from the garden, mopping his red face after trying to explain the burst pipe to the man from the Water Board. He sat down beside Katy, jogging her arm and spilling hot chocolate on the blanket.

"Let's give her another chance, Katy," he said. "She saved Tommy's life, you know. And possibly even yours as well. She had you both out of there in seconds. Your mum saw it happen from an upstairs window."

"I nearly had a heart attack," grumbled Katy's mum, rubbing at the chocolate stain with a cloth and sending Tommy diving for cover under the sofa. She took Katy's cup from her hand and tucked the blanket more snugly round her. "But to be fair Jane only made the pool to stop herself from drying out. She really does need to swim every day, or all her skin flakes off. It wasn't her fault you fell in, was it?"

"I suppose not," mumbled Katy.

"Let her stay, love," said Katy's dad, and Katy sighed. Throwing out somebody who had just fished you out of the pond was a pretty rotten thing to do, she supposed.

The door opened and Jane came in. She shuffled her webbed feet on the carpet, a strange gleam in her eyes.

"I've got something to tell you," she said. "I don't think you're going to like it."

"Sit down, Jane," said Katy's dad, peering about for his glasses which he'd lost somewhere in all the excitement. "Katy has something to tell you, too. Haven't you, Katy?"

Katy stared at Jane for a moment and took a deep breath. "You needn't go home just yet," she said grudgingly. "You can stay if you like."

Jane's face brightened at once. "It's a good job you've changed your mind," she said with a grin. "I can't leave anyway. That's what I was coming to tell you. The spaceship battery's flat."

She glanced towards the window where the rain still drummed against the pane. "It's this rotten weather," she told the astonished family. "My computer has just worked out that the solar batteries need two weeks of your Earth sunshine to charge enough for take-off. Without that I won't be going anywhere."

Katy's dad's mouth had dropped open like a frog catching flies.

"Crikey!" he said. "With the summer we're having you could be here for months."

The family gazed at one another in silence for a moment. Katy's mum gave a little cough.

"We might even have to take her with us to Gran's," she said faintly.

Katy began to giggle helplessly at the very thought.

"I can hardly wait," she said, moving over to make room for Jane on the sofa beside her.